An Introduction to
LITERACY
TEACHING

ALBSU
Adult Literacy & Basic Skills Unit

Foreword

"An Introduction to Literacy Teaching" was first published in February 1980 by the Adult Literacy Unit and quickly became established as an essential basic handbook for adult literacy tutors. It was produced by a group of experienced adult literacy practitioners and edited by ALU. I believe that "An Introduction to Literacy Teaching" continues to provide both a useful introduction for new tutors as well as a valuable source of information and ideas for the more experienced. Essentially this edition remains the same as the original although we have corrected some of the addresses and titles which appear towards the end of the book.

Alan Well, Director
Adult Literacy and Basic Skills Unit

The Working Group

Gillian Anciano
Basic Education Organiser,
London Borough of Newham

Rosemary Eggar
Organiser,
Cambridge House Literacy Scheme, London

Christine Higgott
formerly, Adult Literacy Organiser,
Thanet, Kent

Susan Jones
Adult Literacy Organiser,
London Borough of Barking

Anna Rossetti
Materials Development Officer,
Basic Skills Unit, National Extension College

Cal Weatherald
Adult Literacy Organiser,
Highbury Manor Adult Education Institute,
Inner London Education Authority

Contents

Part 1
Some Aspects of Adult Literacy

Everyone at some time or another needs to develop existing skills or acquire new ones. This may involve anything from learning to type, changing the oil in a car, speaking a foreign language, being a parent, or learning to read and write.

Many choices and opportunities in life are denied to you, if you are not literate enough to do the things you want to do. Both at work or as a member of society it is difficult to take advantage of opportunities if you doubt your ability to cope with the written communication this may involve. Perhaps the best way to illustrate this is to think of all the times in the day that you read or write something and imagine what effect it would have on your life if you couldn't read or write very well.

The good reader

Fluent readers do not generally stop to think about how they read and exactly what processes are involved. Most reading involves a number of strategies, and is not just a matter of reading one / word / after / another / until / we / have / lost / the / sense / of / what / we / are / reading /. Reading often involves glancing at headlines, looking for key words and main points, reading enough to get the gist of a passage, guessing at unfamiliar words, and looking things up for specific information or detail. Only rarely is it necessary to break down individual words in order to get the meaning of a passage.

Is literacy necessary?

Many people who have difficulty with reading and writing cope in one way or another and lead full and interesting lives. Although it may sometimes be a nuisance, difficulty with reading or writing does not affect their daily lives so much that they want to improve their literacy skills. It may be that they can ask friends or relations or avoid reading and writing as much as possible. Others will confidently admit their difficulty, even in public, and get someone else to fill in the form or read the notice. However, for many adults the stigma attached to inadequate literacy becomes too much to bear and a decision has to be made to do something about it.

It would be foolish to pretend that deciding to join a literacy scheme is just like dropping in at the local pottery class. The decision is a very personal one influenced by a whole range of factors and usually thought out quite carefully beforehand. Often it is prompted by the fear of being branded illiterate.

> "When she saw I was having difficulty spelling the numbers, this bank clerk said to me, 'People who can't manage to fill out a cheque properly oughtn't to be allowed a cheque book.' I felt awful."

Sometimes it is a general desire to feel 'normal', the same as everyone else. Some people get tired of always depending on someone else — or else their circumstances change and suddenly they have to become more independent.

Students

Adult literacy students are as varied as other students and there is no such thing as a typical student. Students are of all ages and come from a wide range of occupations and backgrounds bringing with them an equally wide range of skills and experiences. These are just a few we have met and worked with:-

Dave, 29, is married with a young family and works as a quality controller in a sugarbeet factory. His supervisor has been hinting at promotion but Dave has put him off so far as he is worried about his spelling. "I want to get on in my job and provide for my family, but all the better jobs mean a lot of paperwork. I don't want my daughters to grow up and find out I can't spell."

Paul, a traveller, wishes to settle down, marry and find a steady job. He hopes to train as a welder and needs to be able to read and write and do arithmetic in order to be accepted on a Government Training Course. "My fiancee tries to help but she gets a bit impatient with me when I don't remember things. It's a bit difficult. People think you're stupid."

Laura, 63, is an unmarried Polish woman who came to Britain before the war. She is now retired and attends classes regularly. "I'm tired of other people having to help me when I want to write letters to the hospital or to the gas people. I want to be able to do it myself."

Sandra, 31, is married and has a family. She has recently begun work again as a residential social worker. She is anxious about her ability to spell and express herself adequately. "I have to write reports every weekend. I feel very embarrassed about showing them to anyone. I read lots but just can't express myself on paper."

Albert, 55, is a hospital porter. He came to Britain from Jamaica 20 years ago. He can read and write well enough to cope with his job. "My daughters said to me, 'Dad, why don't you do something about your reading and writing?' I think they're right. I think it's time I improved myself."

Perhaps the main thing that these students all share is that they are making a decision about the direction they want their lives to move in, whether in relation to other people or to their own development. The things they say illustrate the lack of confidence felt by most adult literacy students and often the first task of any tutor is to help the student to become more self-confident. With this in mind, it is particularly important for a student to know that the feelings of anxiety he or she may have about learning to read and write are taken seriously.

Tutors

Tutors as well as students usually begin with some uncertainties. After all, there is no single set course book and no fixed curriculum, so it may seem rather like launching out without a boat. However, talking with the student can provide points from which a start can be made. Students often have an interest or specific need and it makes sense to capitalise on this when beginning teaching. These are just a few of the things tutors we know have said in describing how they found a place to begin:-

> "She was a very keen Labour party worker and as she talked I was impressed with how well informed she was. She wanted to do more writing about these interests and first wanted to work on spelling people's names."

> "I asked him about his job and started to write down some of the things he said, but that was rather a mistake! He was bored at work and certainly didn't want to spend his evenings on it. Once we got talking about films, though, it was much better."

6

"I was pleased that he liked talking about driving as I was learning to drive and was a bundle of nerves about it all. He'd had years of experience on the road and obviously could cope with any situation. His advice helped and calmed me down a lot, and we started work on 'advice notes', where we wrote down the things he would say to a new driver, based on his experience."

Experiences of learning

When students have very little confidence in their ability to learn, it can be useful to spend some time talking about successful learning they have experienced. A list of these experiences, both in and out of school, might cover a wide range and include such things as:-

- learning job routines and processes at work
- learning about bringing up children and dealing with their problems
- learning to drive
- remembering addresses and telephone numbers
- learning other school subjects, perhaps practical ones like woodwork or needlework
- learning to do household jobs

It may also be useful to look at other learning experiences which have not been successful, particularly as we often learn from failing at a task and students need to be aware that this is a part of all learning. Unwillingness to try, and risk failure, is often negative and means we only attempt learning things we feel sure of succeeding in.

How do you learn?

You may find it useful to think of one or two of your own learning experiences which did not prove successful, as we have done below. The idea is to try to pinpoint what were the main reasons for failure. Our experiences ranged from car maintenance to learning French and the reasons we came up with as to why we failed included:-

- low opinion of our own ability
- lack of confidence
- lack of stimulation, leading to boredom
- feeling of stress
- poor relationship with teacher

- change of teacher
- no support from others
- distraction of other things going on
- too much use of jargon
- feelings of competition
- too much information at once
- poor memory

By talking about these factors you can begin to see how learning is affected by many things other than intelligence. It is also a relief for the student to find that other people have failed for similar reasons. As one tutor said,

> "I've just realised why I never play darts. It's the scoring that I'm scared of. My friends have been playing for years and have no trouble adding up the scores really quickly. I guess I just don't want to show myself up."

Talking about learning

In talking about previous learning experiences it is useful to consider a number of questions such as:-

- did it help to watch a demonstration?
- was repetition useful?
- did illustrations help?
- how often and how long were the lessons? (if any)
- was there a lot of talking with other people?
- did you use tricks or sayings to help you remember?

Although many of the methods discussed may not be suitable for improving reading and writing, talking things over will help to show that there are a number of ways of learning. If one strategy or method is not suitable then another one can always be tried.

It is also particularly important to recognize the difference between understanding and remembering. You could, for instance, look up a new recipe, understand the ingredients, the amounts and the method but until you had made the dish a number of times, you couldn't say you really knew how to do it. Similarly, it may be relatively easy for a literacy student to understand the value of using context — that is, leaving a word which is giving trouble, reading on and then guessing the difficult word from the meaning of the sentence — but it could be quite some time before it becomes automatic.

You may know little about what the student already knows and which approaches are most suitable. Some students learn most easily by *looking* at words, some by *saying* them and others by getting the feel of the *writing*, and for some, all these methods will be helpful. It is probably a good strategy to try all three ways so that students can decide which work best for them. Robert, for example, had written 'chonsir' for chosen. He realised it was wrong but couldn't correct it. When he was shown the correct version, he looked at it for a while and then wrote 'chorsn'. Another attempt produced 'chonsir' again. After being given the word written on a card and cut in two, he studied the two parts, saying them to himself, wrote them, then wrote the whole word correctly. It has taken him some time to accept this rather lengthy procedure but he now recognises that 'just looking' won't do for him.

Groups and one-to-one

Some students find it easier to work with one tutor, in a quiet atmosphere where there is less distraction and more individual attention. Others prefer being in a group and sharing problems and successes with the other group members. Groups are obviously organised differently depending on the students and the way the tutor likes teaching. However, it is worth remembering that the organisation of the group will affect how people relate to one another as well as the content of the work.

If you are working in a group, you will be in a good position to encourage students to work together and help each other. You may also be able to develop work based on broad areas of interest to the whole group although it is obviously important that follow-up work is related to the needs of the different students. Some groups use a piece of group writing to provide a basis for work for individual students at different levels.

Working as a tutor with a student on a one-to-one basis means that planning work, devising material and keeping records will need to be discussed and agreed between both of you. In a group, these tasks are more likely to be shared with other tutors and students.

The right pace

This is something that tutors and students learn by experience. At first, the time spent on concentrated work might be quite short, increasing over the weeks. Changes of activity are particularly important in literacy teaching especially if students are tired after a day's work and lots of short but varied tasks are preferable to one lengthy concentrated piece of work. It is not always easy, of course, to know when to repeat an activity or when to leave it for a while and introduce something fresh, although with experience these decisions should become easier. If in doubt, the simple thing is to ask the students how they feel about it and take their advice.

There will be times when no new learning seems to be taking place, when a student appears to have reached a plateau and cannot move forward. This is quite usual, and probably means that the student needs to review and practise what has gone before, to consolidate learning. Discussing this, and seeing it as a positive rather than negative time will help to avoid discouragement.

The importance of building confidence cannot be overestimated, and this may be where you see the first and most noticeable progress. As students gain in self-confidence, they feel more able to tackle different tasks, and to work independently.

Part 2
Some Practical Approaches to Teaching

Beginning teaching – Four students. **WILF** Word matching – Key words – Sight words – Words within words – Sounds – Cloze Procedure – Handwriting. **SUSAN** Using a dictionary – Classifying Information – Punctuation – Skimming – Scanning – Proof-reading – Drafting and Editing. **ANN** Alphabetical order – Spelling – Homophones – Hearing Reading – Letter Writing – Synonyms. **RAY** Form-filling – Access Skills – Classification – Abbreviations – Notes and Memos – Maps and Plans.

Literacy is about reading *and* writing — that is, understanding and using written language. For most things, we need to be able to use both reading and writing together — but as separate skills, they need to be learnt differently.

Fluent readers do not read individual words, but follow the general flow of what they are reading in order to understand it. When you meet an unfamiliar word in reading you generally see it in the context of the whole passage and by using that context you can 'guess' the word, or you can omit it or break it into smaller parts.

Fluent writers build up sentences from previous knowledge of words and sounds. Unfamiliar words can often be built up by adapting known word patterns to the new word. Context in this case is not going to help and you need to know what the common patterns are. Further, visual memory plays an important part in remembering how to spell most words.

Most students will want to work on both reading and writing.

Beginning teaching

A lot of tutors ask, "Where do I start?". A student will not be at one specific level. He may have picked up knowledge through his work, hobbies, or home life and be quite competent at some complex aspects of literacy, whereas in other areas quite simple tasks may present a problem. For instance, Tony works in a paint depot and can recognise the names of the colours, not only reds, blues and greens but also Hogarth, vermilion and magenta. Many adults who are improving their literacy skills have similar pockets of knowledge.

One way to overcome the problem of how to start is to base your work on students' own spoken or written words, and on the things they have to read or write. All the students in our examples are working in this way.

Four students

In this section we are going to look at four students at different levels. In each case there is a description by the tutor of what happened, followed by some points we think are important, including a summary of what techniques the tutor was using and why, and finally some ideas on how the work could develop.

Some of the ideas are for individual work, others could be used with either groups or individuals. All of them can be adapted.

WILF

"Wilf did not believe he could read any words. After talking to me he realised he could recognise some words in their appropriate context, for example, 'bus stop' on the sign. In further conversation he said he backed horses sometimes and could pick out the horse 'April the Seventh' because it was his birthday. From the conversation we agreed to work on the sentences:

> My name is Wilf Green
>
> and I live in London.
>
> My birthday is on April the Seventh.

I read the sentences to Wilf several times, and then I asked him to read them with me. We did this a couple of times and then I read more and more quietly until Wilf was reading by himself. He had another go by himself, but stopped at the word 'birthday'. I suggested he read on and try to work out the word from the rest of the sentence. Wilf was still unsure so I asked him what happened on April the seventh and then he was able to work out the word.

Once Wilf felt fairly certain of the sentences I made a second copy of them. In this instance I wrote the words out, but in later activities Wilf wrote them out himself. Through all the following work Wilf knew he could refer to the master copy of the sentences whenever he wanted and practise on his own.

I put the sentences on to separate pieces of card, and asked Wilf to match them to the master card.

and I live in London.

My name is Wilf Green

My birthday is on April the Seventh.

My name is Wilf Green

and I live in London.

My birthday is on April the Seventh.

He was able to put the sentences into the right order very quickly and write them into his book. He found that he was able to write a few of the words without having to refer continually to the master card.

We then took each sentence separately and I cut the card into individual words. Wilf read the sentence and I asked him to point out specific words. Then I moved the words around and asked Wilf to put them in the order of the sentence. Whenever he had difficulty he knew he could refer to the master card.

Wilf	My	is	name	Green

Master card

My name is Wilf Green

We did this with each sentence, and at each stage, Wilf was able to practise by himself.

The next stage was to remove one word card from each sentence. I asked Wilf to say which word fitted into which sentence. He then wrote the sentences putting in the missing words. This work was spread over several sessions. Other things we did during this time included learning his name and address. Wilf could recognise his name but not his address. I wrote the words on to a master card and we did the same sort of things I have just described.

Later, Wilf tried making up new sentences using the words he had learnt. In the absence of a master card Wilf could gain immediate feedback through another simple checking device: by marking numbers on the reverse side of the cards, he could check whether he had got the sentence in the right order, for example

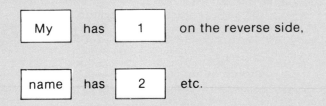

My	has	1	on the reverse side,

name	has	2	etc.

Once Wilf had built up a sight vocabulary, and could recognise a reasonable number of everyday words, we began some work on sounds. From the words he already knew I selected three that began with the same sound, for example, birthday, but, bus, and wrote them on cards. I read them aloud and got him to say the word several times to hear the sound at the beginning. Then he

14

tried to think of some other words that began with the same sound and the same letter. I wrote them all down and Wilf looked at each of them to decide whether it belonged to the group. We talked about the words, and he chose the ones he wanted to read. We then worked out some sentences with the words in and used them for reading and matching exercises. Later on we did the same thing with sounds at the end of the word, for example, London, Green, seven. These were more difficult to hear and I had to emphasise the final sound. We intend to carry on, using longer pieces of writing, building up Wilf's vocabulary and showing him more techniques for working out words."

Points to notice

1. Wilf didn't believe he could read any words and really lacked confidence in himself. By talking to him and helping him to realise he could actually read something already the tutor was able to boost his confidence straight away. In fact Wilf could read some words, and probably more than was shown in the example. He just didn't think he could.

2. The tutor wrote down what Wilf said. It's not always easy to get a student to say something when they know it's going to be written down — it makes you seem like a policeman! It's also an unfamiliar way of learning. You just have to be bold and write down absolutely anything he says, including: "I don't know what to say".

Sometimes, when something interesting crops up, you can scribble it down quickly and then complete and correct it with the student's help. "I wrote that down quickly because I thought it was interesting. Can you see if you think I've got it right? — or would you like to change it or add to it?"

3. The way to use this language experience approach with a beginning reader should be clear from the example. We just want to draw your attention to a couple of things:

— *don't change the language.* If your student says 'aint', write 'aint'. If singulars and plurals are mixed up, leave it as it is. That's not what you're dealing with at the moment and it would only cause confusion to introduce these extra points — apart from undermining confidence and understanding.

— *use short lines.* Most sentences break naturally into phrases:

> "My name is Wilf Green
>
> and I live in London"

This makes it easier for a beginning reader because it gives him a chance to pause without losing the sense and allows him to tackle small bits at a time. This is called 'line-breaking'.

4. From the beginning Wilf has been encouraged to use several techniques to work out unknown words.

— leaving the word out and coming back to it
— guessing from the words around it and from his previous knowledge
— using the sounds as a clue

When we read, we use similar strategies, whereas the use of sounds to decode in reading is fairly rare. In fact, it is probably true that we recognise the sounds that letters, and combinations of letters, make because we are already competent readers, rather than the other way round. It seems to us that learning sounds is not the first priority, and doesn't help the beginning reader to make a confident start.

5. You should explain to the student what you are doing and why. Unless the student knows the reason for doing a task he is unlikely to be very interested or to learn effectively from it. You will probably already know this from your own learning experiences.

Work which could be developed

Wilf needs a lot of individual work at this stage. However, in a group situation, good use can be made of a tape recorder and self-checking material for the student to practise with on his own. Some of the activities outlined below could be adapted for practice on tape, such as cloze exercises. A tape can also act as 'tutor' in some instances by providing feedback for the student to check his own work.

Word matching. Use some words from the student's vocabulary. Write each one on two pieces of card using only five or six pairs at a time. Put all the cards on the table, face up. Select one and name it. Ask the student to find the matching card and repeat the word.

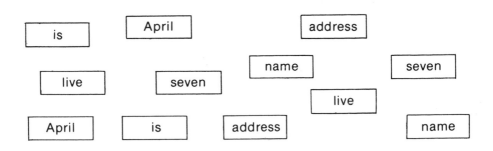

At a later stage, when the student is familiar with the words, put all the cards on the table face up, and ask the student to choose and name a pair of cards. Once the student is absolutely confident with these words, you can play a game. Put all the cards on the table face down and take turns in selecting two cards. If they match, name and keep them. The winner is the one with most pairs at the end. It is important that games like this are introduced only once the words have been thoroughly learnt, so that winning is a matter of luck with the cards, not a question of reading ability. Otherwise the tutor would always win.

Key words. These are small, common words that recur in all reading and writing. Although they are a relatively small group of words, they are particularly important and are difficult to learn by sounding out (try sounding out 'said' and 'they').

The following 32 words make up on average ⅓ of all the words we read or write:-

a all and are as at be but for had have he him his I in is it not of one said so that the they to was we with you

Along with these additional words, the total 100 words make up on average ½ of all the words we read or write:

about an back been before big by call came can come could did do down first from get go has her here if into just like little look made make me more much must my new no now off old only or other our out over right see she some their them then there this two up want well went were what when where which who will your

(From: J McNally and W Murray: 'Key Words to Literacy and the Teaching of Reading' Schoolmaster Publishing Company.)

You could use word matching (see above), or games based on snap, bingo or dominoes. The number of words used at any one time should not exceed six or eight.

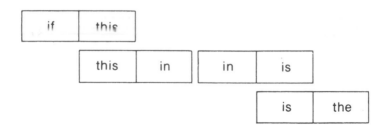

In a newspaper article the student could underline a specific key word each time it appears.

Theatres heading for 'worst slump'

by Charles Spencer

THE lights are going out all over the West End. Her Majesty's Theatre is dark, The Queen's is dark, The Shaftesbury is dark, The Royalty is dark.

Now Ian Albery, a leading West End producer and theatre manager has warned that the situation is likely to get worse in the months ahead.

"One fifth of the theatres in the West End may be dark soon. I think it has been apparent since this time last year that the theatre was heading for very serious trouble, but last Spring I said the big trouble was going to be after Christmas in 1980. We've been living on borrowed productions and borrowed time."

Albery believes the commercial theatre is probably facing its worst crisis since the thirties. "The only comparable period was in the mid to late fifties when black and white television came in in a big way. You would have to go back to then to find a comparable state of decline."

He says a whole host of factors are to blame for the bleak

IAN ALBERY

outlook—the hefty increase in the rate of VAT which has pushed seat prices up, the collapse in the American tourist trade, above all perhaps inflation. "Inflation in the theatre is a terrible thing. We are labour intensive and 90 per cent of our costs are labour costs.

"It's like a circle. These things are chasing each other's tail. They all inter-relate."

The circle is a vicious one. Because of the economic difficulties facing the theatre, producers are finding it increasingly hard to find good new plays along with the financial backers who could help re-vitalise the West End. "There is a dearth of new product and producers can't find the money to put new plays on, anyway. The investors have caught a cold so many times they are getting shy about putting up the money."

Vicious

At present only one in five shows in the West End makes a profit," added Mr Albery. Two in five break even while the other two make a big loss. But soaring costs have whittled away the profit margins on the successful shows, making it more and more difficult for them to make enough money to cover the flops.

"I don't say we are actually going to see theatres pulled down in the next 12 months, but I think we will have theatres closed for weeks and months at a time and the staff will be laid off."

His fellow producer John Gale views the future with similar pessimism. "It is appalling at the moment. I can't ever remember it being as bad as this. I think we will see less and less live theatre in the future. There are theatres shut already and half the theatres that are open should be shut only it's cheaper to pay the losses rather than shut them completely," he said.

He added that in the present gloomy climate he had no plans to stage new plays himself.

The producer Michael Codron takes a brighter view however. "I always tend to be a bit of a Micawber and think something will turn up. There's no doubt that all of us are going through a testing time, but there are new productions coming up. It always seems to be bad in January and February—maybe these difficulties will make us more adventurous."

Diet

"What we have got to do is win the British theatre is woo the British audience back," said Ian Albery.

He believes stimulating, challenging plays are the way to do this rather than the current diet of musical revivals and jaded formula comedies.

The key words also need to be spelt. You could use exercises that involve writing the words in a sentence.

> I ran..........the door.   She..........some tea..........went home.

Also use exercises which involve putting missing letters into a word.

> sa...d   w...   y...u   w...s   bac...   bef......e

Sight words.   These are words that the student sees a lot in everyday life, at work, in the street, shopping. Each person has a slightly different group of words, though some are common to us all, *Exit, No Smoking, Toilets*, etc. They are words that are more often read than written.

You could write the sight words the student wants to remember on to pieces of card. Hold them up for him to look at quickly and help him to build up his recognition of them.

However, recognising a lot of these words depends on the style they are written in. A lot of signs are in capital letters or use a particular typographic style. They are also more easily remembered in their appropriate context, for example,

Where possible, use the same style and point out the different ways they can be written.

Words within words.   Ask the student to find known words inside longer unfamiliar words, for example,

All these activities rely fairly heavily on visual skills and only a certain number of words can be committed to memory in this way.

Sounds.   Reading work involving sounds may be helped by matching and grouping activities. By concentrating on one sound, at the beginning, in the middle or at the end of words, a list of words can be produced. Make up some nonsense sentences with the student, for example,

---

"Ned is not my nephew's name, my nephew's name is Norman."

"The rain in Spain falls mainly on the plain."

You can then cut up the sentences into individual words for various games — memory games, dominoes, bingo, snap — or simply sort them into groups and add more words. Try making up other nonsense sentences.

To be meaningful, the sounds need to be used as part of words and phrases.

Cloze Procedure.   When we read, we are getting the meaning from the words on the page. It doesn't matter if we can't read every word as we can omit the odd word and still get the gist of it. This is an activity that some people see as 'cheating' but, in fact, it is a strategy for coping with unknown words. The fluent reader probably uses this method more than any other.

You can take a passage and leave out some words and then work together to discuss the sort of words the writer might have used, bearing in mind that there are no right or wrong answers.

A point to remember when preparing this activity is not to delete too many words. The more words deleted, the more difficult it is to understand what's written.

My name is Wilf Green. I live in ....

My birthday is on April the I

like horse racing. I back a horse every

week if .... can. Sometimes I .... something.

20

Cloze is particularly useful for readers who are reluctant to read past an unknown word as it encourages them to read on and then guess the missing word.

You could also try the following with students:

- Delete key words. After he has identified the missing words, the student can practise writing and spelling them.

- Omit words that contain the same sound. You can set clues from discussing the writing and words first — or by providing certain letters in the word as well as the correct number of spaces. For example, **day**:

> We...........have to..........to see the May.........display.

- In a group, students can write their own material, leaving out words for other students to guess.

Handwriting. The amount of work to be done on handwriting will depend on the writer's ability. Some students' writing is fine and they are quite happy with the presentation. Others worry that their handwriting shows how bad they are at reading and writing. To cope with each situation, you need to know the student's feelings about his own writing in order to offer the most appropriate support. You also need to ensure the student can read what *you* write.

Some habits will be hard to break and you need to consider whether it is necessary to do so. Will forming a certain letter the 'wrong' way make it more tiring for the student, if he is writing for any length of time? Might *his* way make the learning of joined writing more complicated?

As much as possible, work from the student's knowledge and build on it. Encourage the student to proof-read his own writing to pick out features he feels need to be improved. Only in circumstances where the formation of the letters is getting in the way of the real reasons for writing, i.e. to communicate, should you consider altering radically the way the student writes.

For a student who writes well but is not happy with the style, it might be useful to collect together a wide variety of examples of handwriting from tutors. The student may then begin to see that his own style is no less legible than most people's.

By not starting to alter someone's handwriting immediately, you may find that he alters it himself just by doing more writing.

A student who is a beginning reader and writer may use large and small letters indiscriminately. Is this due to nerves? Is the student unaware of the use of capital (upper case) and small (lower case) letters? Does the student have difficulty in discriminating between the lower case **b** and **d** or **p** and **q** so uses the upper case equivalents? What about the spacing between words? Having sorted out the answers to these questions and others that you have in mind, a few activities need to be planned. They might include some of the following:

□ Write out a reference alphabet in large (upper case) and small (lower case) letters, for example, **Aa, Bb,** etc.

□ Work on one group of letters that derive from one basic shape, for example,

c   c a d e g o q

These letters can then be used to form words that the student can trace and write below. Make sure the size of the writing lines is not too close. Encourage the student to over-emphasise the size to begin with in order to feel the shape of the letter.

□ Do matching activities for upper and lower case letters — individual letters on cards, handwritten, typed, letraset. Ask the student to write down letters in small or capital letters which he can then check from cards.

□ For joined writing, some basic patterns could be introduced to help the student feel the flow of shapes. Use a variety of writing materials — pencil. felt tip, plain paper, wide lined paper, etc.

SUSAN

"Susan has lived in the same area all her life. She has read several books by other students about their early lives and feels she would like to write about her own experiences. Our scheme hopes to publish her writing as a book. She wanted to find out a bit about the history of her area so we went to the library.

Susan was rather shy about asking the librarian where to find things so I asked the librarian for guidance a few times to show her that it is the normal thing to do, and she soon lost her fear. We also looked at the catalogue and Susan is now learning how it works.

Once we were in the right section of the library it became obvious that Susan couldn't read every single book, so she had to learn to **skim** and **scan**.

Skimming just meant getting the feel of a book. We talked about how we should go about picking up the main points, at least enough to see which bits we wanted to look at more closely, and it wasn't easy. Later we worked for some time on newspapers and magazines where the headlines and pictures made it much easier.

Scanning was useful because she was looking for particular bits in a local history book she had read before. She found it quite easy to flick through and find the bit she wanted with the help of the index, contents and chapter headings, but I thought there was a danger she would get bogged down in all this and not get started with her writing.

She didn't want me to write it down for her because dictating everything to me would be too slow, but she didn't want to write it herself. She thought if she wrote it herself she'd lose the thread of what she was saying because she'd keep worrying about the spelling, and therefore tend to use words she could spell, instead of saying what she really wanted.

I suggested she dictate it on to a tape recorder. She was a bit nervous at first and we both thought our voices sounded silly. In *the end what we did was to leave it on while we talked naturally and after a while we got used to it. Now she dictates a bit at a time and transcribes it herself.*

When she comes to a word she doesn't know, she can do a number of things:

— look it up in a dictionary
— have a go at it
— ask me or someone else

Here is a short extract from what she wrote:

'I've lived in the country all my life. My father worked on a farm looking after horses. He only got 4 shillings a week and we lived in a tied cottage. That means that our house belonged to the farmer. We were very poor, mother had to go out to work on the farm too, planting, staking and picking. In the summer there was picking of strawberries and raspberries, and in the autumn there was apples and potatoes. All us kids used to go with her. We started going when we were quite young. We used to help too, so as to earn some money. I missed a lot through working on the land.' "

Points to notice

1. Everything was based on what the student wanted to do. Although Susan only had one purpose — to write about her experiences — a lot of other subsidiary purposes were identified — including using the library, developing reading techniques and improving spelling.

2. The tutor and student did a lot of talking, and every stage of the work was discussed — not only what to do, but also the best way of doing it.

3. Although Susan could read well enough to be able to work out the meaning of a piece of writing she was given, she didn't know all the uses for reading. Susan was learning ways of using her reading and developing skills such as skimming, scanning, finding and storing information.

4. Although lots of people are self conscious about using a tape recorder, it doesn't usually take long to get over that stage. People just aren't used to

hearing themselves speak, and recording *does* make your voice sound funny. A tape recorder is a valuable teaching aid — mainly because it can make the student independent of the tutor. There are some small technical problems you might have to sort out, like having the microphone in the right place, background noise, etc., but a little experimentation should sort out these problems quite quickly.

5. Susan was shy of asking the librarian to help. A lot of students think asking people is a sign of stupidity, or that if they ask they are revealing the fact that they can't read or write very well. By example, you can help to get the student past that hurdle.

Work which could be developed — for an individual or a group.

Using a Dictionary.   Students may be wary of using dictionaries, not knowing the right technique or being confused with phonetic spellings, notes about derivation and small print. It is worth pointing out that a dictionary can only be used to check spelling if you have some idea of how to spell the word.

You could try some of the following with students:

□ Some students find it useful to build up their own dictionary of words that are important to them, and these could be listed in a notebook according to the initial letter but otherwise not strictly in alphabetical order. An address notebook is useful for this.

□ Together, look at a number of different dictionaries to compare size of print, layout, etc. People tend to have their personal preferences, so let the student select the one he finds easiest to use.

□ Practise alphabetical order by opening the dictionary at a given letter. The student then says which letter comes before and which after it. Students can practise this on their own or in a group and check for themselves.

□ Produce word cards to be put in alphabetical order.

— with different first letters

tin
book
group
nation

— with the same first letter

> book
> big
> band
> bell

— with the same first two letters

> brown
> bread
> brick
> brand

— with the same first three letters

> brown
> brother
> broken
> broad

▫ Give a page number in the dictionary, and several words from that page, each on separate cards. Ask the student to find the words on the page, then put the cards into alphabetical order. Again this can be a self-checking exercise.

▫ Give the first and last words of a page on cards, then a selection of other words. Ask the student to decide if these words come within the page or not, then check with the real page.

▫ Give a definition. The student then suggests possible words to fit the definition and checks in a dictionary.

▫ Try comparing meanings given in two or three dictionaries.

Classifying Information.   Quite a lot of useful work on classification can be done through discussion. For example you could try some of the following:

▫ Which words mean the same?

> loud
> annoying
> noisy
> rowdy

▫ Which word describes all the others?

> lettuce
> potato
> carrot
> vegetable

- The same activities could be repeated with words on cards, or words together with pictures (some cut from catalogues) to classify into groups such as shops, foods, trades and jobs, cars etc. according to students' interests and needs. Headings could be given or left for the students to supply.

- Specific tasks can be given. For example, ask the student to find a particular service in Yellow Pages.

- Help the student to devise a personal storage system. For example, he might want a storage system for recipes or household bills.

Punctuation. For the beginning reader the use of full stops can be introduced with very early work. These simply set markers for the end of statements. Later the use of capital letters at the beginnings of sentences can be practised.

Rather than attempting initially to develop an awareness of the niceties and nuances of using punctuation, only those punctuation marks which are essential should be pointed out, for example, full stops and question marks.

Later, commas and quotation marks can be discussed and later still exclammation marks, semi-colons, colons and other forms of punctuation.

However, this should not form a rigid sequence of teaching. A student may notice quotation marks, for instance, quite early on in his reading and ask what they are — in which case this might be developed. Other punctuation marks, like colons, may never be needed.

Try some of the following with the students:

- Passages can be read for meaning and then afterwards read consciously, noting the use of punctuation. You can discuss the effect particular marks have on the meaning of the passage.

- Sentences can be read out loud to illustrate the effect of punctuation on intonation as well as meaning, for example:

> Get out (the cutlery)
> Get out!
> Get out?

- For further practice, sample passages can be rewritten leaving out most or all punctuation. The student can then add the punctuation he thinks appropriate and check his version with the original. The differences — not always errors — can form the basis for discussion.

27

Skimming. This means just glancing through a piece of reading to get a general idea of what it is about. You could practise this with the student by some of the following:

- Read a short paragraph and select the most appropriate title from three or four provided.

- Read a short paragraph and suggest a title.

- Read newspaper articles and note down the main points.

Scanning. This means looking for specific details. Here are some ways you can offer practice:

- Pose questions asking for a specific detail from a short text, for example, "What colour was the car?"

- Ask questions concerned with the whereabouts of certain information, for example, "On which page is the word 'bank'?"

Proof-reading. Having written something, it is always wise to read it through to check the spelling and content of the material. This is an activity that all of us use quite frequently. When we write, we have to think of what we want to write as well as how to put those words on paper. If we are thinking a lot faster than we are writing it may be that words get left out.

By proof-reading, these words can be added, and other words can be changed to more appropriate ones. Some spellings can also be checked in this way.

It may take a bit of practice to read what is actually written rather than what is thought to be there, and for a student at the beginning level, it may be useful for the tutor to write the piece out so that the student can proof-read his writing against a master copy.

Drafting and Editing. By discussion, attempt to dispel the notion that 'literate' people can produce a final version at the first go (indeed, novelists, playwrights and poets constantly re-draft and edit their own work.)

You can think of this in two main ways:

- Drafting and editing in terms of *content:*
  The student should ask himself the following questions:

  — what do I *want* to say?

  — which are the key points and which just cloud the issue?

  — which points do I need to add?

  Then he can delete unnecessary points and underline those which need to be expanded.

□ Drafting and editing in terms of *style:*
  The student should consider the following:

  — is the general tone appropriate? (For example, it would be different for an informal letter, a job application, or a letter of complaint).

  — are there particular words or phrases which are not quite right?

A lot of discussion can follow these activities and different views may be expressed.

ANN

> 22, Ringwood Road,
> Devizes
> Wiltshire
> 2nd November 1979
>
> Dear Jenny,
>
> Thank you for your letter. The family are well. How are you keeping? Tom and Sarah send their love. I have started going to classes to learn to spell. One day I might be writing my own letters. What made me decide is that Sarah is going to school and I want to go back to Brownings as a supervisor, but I will have to fill in the forms right.

"This was the start of a letter Ann sent to her sister in America. She found it useful to get me to write down what she said. She read the letter herself and decided what she wanted to change, before writing the letter and sending it.

We discussed the words in the letter, and I asked Ann to pick out some words she was confident she could spell. She chose **Jenny well, Sarah, day.** *Then I asked her to choose some words she would like to learn in the letter, and she chose* **made, might, forms, supervisor.** *We did some work on these words:-*

Made: *Ann often missed the 'e' out.*
We collected together all the words we could think of that had the same sound and were spelt in a similar way. I wrote all the words down and Ann decided whether they should be included in the list. Words such as **rate, came** *and* **tape** *were included but not* **sail** *and* **days.**

Ann was never certain when to add an 'e'. By looking at all the words and comparing them with words such as **mad, hat, tap,** *she found it much easier to decide whether to add an 'e' or not.*

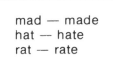

mad — made
hat — hate
rat — rate

Might: *Ann had not met this word in spelling before. We collected words that had the sound and spelling of 'ight' as in* **might.**

fight	tight	light	right

Ann has started to practise, using a dictionary so she can look up the words to check if she was right.

Ann put each of the words in a sentence, and I wrote the sentences down with the 'ight' word omitted. She put in the appropriate word.

You have to .... to get your rights.

It's getting dark, turn on the ....

Forms: *Ann wrote this as 'froms'.*
Ann worked on this word by writing it out several times to feel the

formation of the letters. I then put the word into several sentences for Ann to write.

> "I'm going for some forms."
>
> "Can you form the word forms?"
>
> "Forms, forms forms!"

Supervisor: a long word that Ann felt might be useful in the future. Ann said the word to herself several times and then marked where she felt it divided into parts. I wrote the word on a card for Ann to cut into sections. She cut it $\boxed{su}$ $\boxed{per}$ $\boxed{vi}$ $\boxed{sor.}$ *She moved the pieces around and reformed the word. Then she turned over one section and tried to write out the whole word including the hidden part. She repeated this activity several times until she felt fairly confident about writing the word.*

From dictation Ann wrote out the part of the letter that included the words which she had worked on. We then checked her work with the original to see if there were any mistakes."

Points to notice

1. The tutor asked Ann to choose words she could spell first — thus starting from what the student *can* do rather than what she can't.

2. Ann chose the words she would like to learn. She made the decision as to which words are the most important to her — which she will use again and which she would like to spell. There were probably a lot of words Ann was not sure of spelling but it is not necessary to go through each of them laboriously, or develop each as a teaching point.

3. Ann has started to use a dictionary. A lot of people who are worried about their spelling find it very difficult to look up a word if they don't know how to spell it. Practice with a dictionary does however help with spelling once the student has some idea about the way a dictionary is set out, and the possible spellings of any particular word.

4. The tutor used a variety of techniques to help Ann remember spellings. Different people remember things in different ways, and also different words can be learnt in different ways.

Work which could be developed — for an individual or a group.

Alphabetical order.   The ability to recite the alphabet from A to Z is only of limited value when trying to use a telephone directory or a dictionary. However, in order to locate information which is stored alphabetically it is essential to know where letters stand in relation to one another.

As soon as a working knowledge of order has been established, use it in realistic situations. Work with telephone directories, street guides, indices and dictionaries — after all, they are the reason for learning alphabetical order in the first place.

Some useful activities for teaching alphabetical order are:-

□ Give a few letter cards to be sorted into order, for example, d c e b a, and random letters, not in immediate sequence, for example, v r p n. (Do not use the whole alphabet to begin with.)

□ Give a word in code, where the student has to find the word by using the next letter of the alphabet, for example, uijt (= this) or using the letter before, for example, sghr (= this).

□ Practise finding a particular letter in a dictionary, using the top corner as a guide. If you open the dictionary at **m** and you are looking for **s**, do you move forward or back, and how far?

□ Play 'sevens' with letter cards. One set of alphabet playing-cards are all dealt out. The person with **m** starts, and each player in turn can lay one card down if they have the next one in sequence either forwards or backwards.

□ Use filing cards, as in a filing system, to reinforce and extend early work. It is a simple matter to build up a filing system which can be extended as confidence grows, to include words filed by 2nd and 3rd letters, etc.

All these activities should be made self-checking by providing a copy of the alphabet.

See also page 25 (Using a Dictionary).

Spelling.   Many different senses are involved in spelling and we usually combine various ones to help us. It might be the look of the whole word, the feel of the writing, or the sounds in the word, and what works for you may not work for your student. You cannot teach spelling, you can only show ways of learning, so it is important that the student discovers how he learns best.

Learning to recognise what words look like

Many good spellers operate by knowing when a word does, or does not 'look right'.

□ Encourage looking around to recognise familiar words in the street, at home, at work or on television.

□ Use a personal dictionary for recording words for reference and revision.

□ Try re-arranging a set of jumbled letters or syllables to re-make a word.

□ Complete words where one or more letters have been missed out.

□ Practise recognising short words within longer ones.

NB In each case, opportunity should be given to *write down* the word in order to reinforce the actual *feeling of writing the word.*

Learning to recognise the relationship between sounds and how they are written down

□ Practise recognising and reproducing the separate sound patterns which occur in familiar words. Look at other words in which they occur, for example, 'ight' as in *fight, might, bright, light.*

□ Try breaking words up into syllable patterns. Practise recognising and reproducing the syllable patterns which occur regularly. (For example, dec-or-ation, cor-por-ation, in-form-ation).

□ Build up a knowledge of prefixes (pro-, pre-, ex-, re-, etc.) and suffixes (-ful, -ment, -ate, -ness).

□ Practise using a dictionary to find or check spellings.

□ Develop and use mnemonics (memory techniques) and rhymes which bring together the spelling and the sounds in ways which can easily be remembered. For example,

```
'necessary — one collar and two socks'
```

(The most effective mnemonics are those made up by the student).

□ Identify problem areas in words where the spelling does not match the pronunciation, for example, (w)rite, diff(e)rent. Develop ways of remembering these, for example, special pronunciation — like saying aloud 'govern*m*ent, pronouncing the 'n'.

▢ Practise writing from dictation based on words and sentences which have already been studied.

Looking at whole words — a method particularly useful for words with irregular patterns, for example, days of the week

This method involves:

— reading the word aloud
— naming the letters, paying particular attention to any 'silent' letters
— copying out the word
— proof-reading against the original word
— identifying the difficult parts, for example, Wed*nes*day
— recording in a personal dictionary
— PRACTISING.

Homophones — words with the same sound but different spelling. The spelling of some words which sound the same but are spelt differently can cause problems, such as *there/their, plane/plain, right/write*. If this is the case, the student needs to devise strategies for remembering how to spell each word. Here are some possible approaches for you to try with the student:

▢ Deal with each of a confused pair, for example, *there/their*, on its *own* when it occurs in context — for example "When we got there, it was raining." Practise with other similar examples — Here, there and everywhere." etc.

▢ Make sure a strong new link between words is set up in a way which is clear and easy to remember. Remember it is the student who has to re-link, so a variety of different approaches might be tried, so the student can choose which works for him.

▢ It can help students to remember difficult spelling if together you work out a link between words of the same family, for example,

there	we live there
here	we live here
where	where do you live?

By producing his own sentences, orally and then in writing, using each word correctly, the link will be reinforced for the student.

◻ Find a link with the meaning of the word, for example, to/too,

'too hot' = extra hot, so add an extra 'o'

◻ Link the difficult word with a familiar sentence — this is useful for words which do not relate easily to others in a pattern, for example, *two*/too/to,

"Two's company, three's a crowd"

It is a good idea to keep a log of confusions which regularly arise. Make out small (pocket-size) postcards or file cards, dealing with one version on each side. Give a short explanation with examples, preferably produced by the student. He can refer immediately to the card, pick it out and possibly take it home to work on in a spare moment.

Hearing Reading.   The best reading practice for someone who wants to improve their reading is for them to read silently to themselves. They can spend as long as they like working out words and are not flustered by having someone 'looking over their shoulder'.

The student may enjoy listening to the tutor reading aloud and you might want to set aside regular time for this. This can help the student to follow and enjoy a story.

However, hearing a student read can be useful to help you plan work to develop reading skills, as long as you know what you are looking for. It should not be used as reading practice for the student and you should not interrupt when mistakes are made, unless help is needed. The main thing is that the student is following the text with understanding. Some of the many skills we use in reading are:-

— recognising common words that can't be built up
— guessing words from the other words around them (context cueing)
— using illustrations or other clues to make a good guess
— using sounds to build words
— checking whether our reading makes sense and putting in the right intonation for the meaning.

When you hear a student read, ask yourself:-

— which of these skills are being used
— which of these skills are not being used
— which of these skills need working on.

It would be unrealistic, as well as discouraging to the student, to pick out every mistake. You might focus on one type of error at a time to begin with and concentrate on that.

Always explain to the student what you are doing and why. You might want to make notes to remind you of points to discuss, as long as this does not put the student off. You could then use your notes as a basis for discussion with the student, as well as to help you plan future work together.

Remember that a student may not read aloud as well as he can silently, simply because it is a stressful situation to have someone listening. If the student agrees, both of you may find it useful to record his reading rather than for him to read directly to you. Remember also, that reading aloud is only for *your* benefit and information. For the student gaining meaning from a passage is more important and meaning is likely to be gained best by silent reading.

Letter Writing.   A letter always has a *purpose*, which is closely reflected in the *style*. These two aspects, purpose and style, should be considered together. It is usually helpful to discuss these aspects and perhaps to work out and compose the letter orally before writing it. This can also form a useful group activity, a student or tutor acting as scribe for the group's ideas.

Correspondence to friends or relatives, postcards, greetings on special occasions, many invitations etc. are expressions of a personal message and are therefore written in a spontaneous, informal style. The message itself is more important than the way in which it is conveyed. This kind of letter writing is an ideal way of encouraging students to record events of individual significance, convey feelings or state opinions. Development of technical skills like spelling can then be based on this writing.

Letters ordering goods, asking for or giving information, querying or com-plaining, are in most cases written to people we know only in an official or professional capacity, if at all. It may be important to make a good impression both by what we say and the way we present ourselves. One of the ways of doing this is to observe the set conventions of *formal* letter writing:-

— lay-out:

address of sender	
date	correctly placed
address of person sent to	on the page
beginning	
ending	

— correct spelling and punctuation
— conventions of expression which include

beginnings *Dear Sir,* (to a company or organisation)
Dear Mr, / Mrs. / Ms, (to someone we do not know well but whose name we know)

and **endings** *Dear Sir* ends *Yours faithfully*
Dear Mr. / Mrs. / Ms ends *Yours sincerely.*

The content of a formal letter should be stated *clearly, simply and concisely*, in language as natural as possible. To do this, the writer needs to be quite clear about what he wishes to say. This may involve quite a lot of discussion beforehand and is likely to involve drafting, re-drafting and making a fair copy. You might like to try some of the following activities with students:

▢ Practise different ways of writing the date.

▢ Practise writing out addresses, paying particular attention to punctuation and the way it is set out.

▢ Practise laying out a letter on letter blanks (with lay-out lines already ruled in to create a strong visual impression of the *shape* of a letter).

- Re-order jumbled paragraphs into a logical sequence.

- Fill in 'guided' letters in which certain parts have been omitted for the student to fill in. (This is a useful exercise in a mixed level group, as more or less may be omitted from individual letters.)

- Group a jumbled list of sentences from two different letters (possibly in two different styles) into sentences appropriate to the individual letters.

- Match letters with their answers.

- Re-write badly set out or badly phrased letters.

- Practise writing birthday cards and postcards.

- Keep an individual file of 'model' letters which may come in useful.

- Compose a letter together, tutor and student, or the whole group.

Synonyms. A lot of work done in a group or individually involves 'selecting the right word'. Through discussion, useful work can be done by playing around with words that convey similar meanings. Sometimes there is only one word that will do, but in other cases there may be a variety to choose from.

When writing, students may have to substitute a word of similar meaning for the one they would prefer to use simply because of spelling difficulties. However, this can provide another lead into discussion about synonyms and their usefulness in avoiding repetition.

Some of the following activities may be useful:-

- Use sets of cards with words in four or five 'families' to be sorted into groups by meaning, for example,

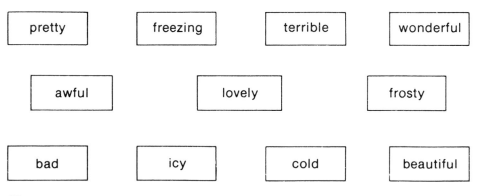

□ Prepare groups of words where the odd one out is to be identified, for example,

```
fast
heavy
quick
speedy
```

□ Use cloze procedure and discuss words with different shades of meaning (see Cloze Procedure, page 20).

□ Rewrite passages, such as newspaper articles, to give practice in finding synonyms.

□ Work with a dictionary and a simple thesaurus or dictionary of synonyms.

□ For those interested crosswords can be used, especially the 'easy' crosswords in newspapers which generally contain a number of synonym clues.

RAY

"Ray has been involved in a car accident, and he brought the accident report form to the group. He wanted to complete the form and send it off, so he read the form with me and filled in what he could. The form asked for two estimates to be submitted.

Ray knew he could get one estimate from his usual garage, but was uncertain about other garages that he could try. The rest of the group joined in our discussion and soon Ray had several addresses to try the next day.

After talking together, all of the students had a go at describing the accident individually as it would appear on the report form. They also drew a sketch map to show where the accident took place, then looked at each other's, asking questions if the description was unclear. For those who were not happy to write their own description, one of the other students or another tutor, wrote their account from dictation."

Points to notice

1. As Ray brought the form with him, this session was not planned in advance. The group tutor, aware of the interest shown by the rest of the group decided to use this topic as a starting point for literacy work. The work that had been planned for the session can be introduced at a later date.

2. The discussion that took place was an important part of the session and formed the starting point for the work that developed. Discussion in a group is not only useful for stimulating ideas for further work however — it can also provide an opportunity for some students to develop their use of language. Some students have difficulty expressing themselves and in a group can, with encouragement, gain in confidence. This in turn can be followed up in written work.

3. This group were keen to show their writing to each other. They have been working together for some time and know that when they read each other's work it is for the meaning of the writing rather than picking up spelling mistakes. Some new students may prefer not to show their writing for the first few weeks, but after a while they usually join in. This is a helpful way for students to gain confidence in reading handwriting.

4. Ray needed to find a second garage and the tutor could have taken this opportunity to develop work on using the Yellow Pages. Most of us tend to ask other people first and this is what happened at the session.

Work which could be developed — for an individual or a group.

Form-filling.   Form filling can be broken down into stages, and discussion should determine what is needed. Practice forms are easily made, or you can usually get some free. A number of practice books for form-filling have also been published.

There are some common features which are worth pointing out:

- Forms use various phrases like *capital letters*, *block letters*, or *print*, which mean the same.
- The section for *Name* is often broken down, for example: surname, Christian names, first name, forenames, given name, other names etc.
- Initials may be needed, rather than forenames written in full.
- Your title can be presented in different ways on different forms, for example,

```
┌─────────────────────────────────────────────────────────────┐
│                                                               │
│   Mr                              ☐ Mr                         │
│   Mrs          CROSS OUT          ☐ Mrs         TICK BOX       │
│   Miss                            ☐ Miss                       │
│   Ms                              ☐ Ms                         │
│                                                               │
└─────────────────────────────────────────────────────────────┘
```

▢ Your address may need to be set out in a certain way, for example,

```
┌─────────────────────────────────────────┐
│                                          │
│   Road ..........................        │
│   Town/City ....................         │
│   County .......................         │
│   Postcode.....................          │
│                                          │
└─────────────────────────────────────────┘
```

▢ Your signature is different from writing out your name or printing, and you need to decide on, and stick to, a signature.

▢ The date can be written, for example, 17th February 1980, or in numbers 17.2.80.

Sometimes it is presented in boxes | 17 | 02 | 80 |

This also applies to date of birth — which often appears on forms as d.o.b.

Often students will want to work on specific forms and it's useful to break each form into a number of manageable steps, and work on each in turn. Practice will probably be needed in fitting the information into the limited space available on most forms.

Access Skills.   Since there is so much printed material available, it is vital that we can *efficiently* gain access to what we need.

First, it is important that we have clear in our own minds the *type* of material we are looking for, for example, guidance on how to grow tomatoes, how to claim supplementary benefit, or how to find out the time a cinema programme starts.

Second, we need to locate the *specific* sources of information. This will vary enormously — it may mean seeking verbal advice (for example, at the Citizen's Advice Bureau) or knowing how to use the library to find appropriate books.

Third, we need to be able to find within a book, magazine or directory the particular piece that interests us. This can involve:-

— using the contents page
— using the index, and knowing alphabetical order and synonyms (see pages 32 and 38).
— using clues within the text (subheadings, bold print, illustrations etc.)
— scanning for key words in order to find the right passage
— skimming the passage to get the gist and to see if it is relevant
— reading in depth.

Try some of the following with students:

☐ Practise using telephone directories to find particular organisations.

☐ Map reading.

☐ Note-taking from verbal or written sources, noting the main points.

☐ Visits to the library where classification systems can be explained.

☐ Practise locating specific topics in books using chapter headings and indices.

☐ Practise scanning passages for 'key' words.

Classification.   Understanding categories speeds up access to the information you require. You could develop this with students by some of the following:

☐ Practise looking in the appropriate column of newspaper adverts.

☐ Get to know the right headings for the Yellow Pages.

☐ Practise finding what you want in a book by using chapter headings.

☐ Work on deciding how to store information so that you can find it in a personal filing system. Items can be listed alphabetically, or according to subject, or according to structure or pattern. Some will need to be listed in more than one place.

Some more activities are suggested on page 26.

Abbreviations.   Abbreviations can take several forms:
— initial letters of words —

```
N = North
DHSS = Department of Health and Social Security
```

— in some cases, the original words may be in another language —

> i.e. = id est (that is)
>
> RSVP = Répondez s'il vous plait (please reply)

— the beginning few letters only of the words may be used —

> Dec = December
>
> Mon = Monday

— the first and last letters of the word may be used —

> wt = weight
>
> hrs = hours

It is always best to deal with the abbreviations as they come up *in context*, — on forms, in classified advertisements etc. — and devise work around this topic. This may include work with students on some of the following:

□ Use the dictionary to look up abbreviations.

□ Look at the main abbreviations connected with one area of interest, for example, weights, directions, addresses.

□ Practise matching words or phrases with their abbreviated forms.

□ Practise using standard abbreviations to write an advertisement or message.

Notes and Memos. When writing notes, we are concerned to communicate main ideas and to record the maximum amount of information in the minimum number of words.

□ Frequently notes are to members of our family, the milkman, or for ourselves. These can be very cryptic — 'Back at 6', '2 pints, please' — and tend to pose few problems, with practice.

□ Other more formal notes are simply brief letters and can be usefully ·

43

introduced as passages to be completed. For example, a letter of absence from school:

Dear ....,

.... will not be at school

.... as she

....

Yours sincerely,

....

□ Taking telephone messages is frequently unnerving for many students. This may not simply be a matter of jotting down the main point but can involve difficulty with spelling names, addresses, etc. Students may need to be reassured that it is perfectly all right to *ask* spellings — "Sorry, I didn't catch that name. Could you spell it please?"

□ Making notes at meetings is a more complex activity. However, practice can be gained by starting with simple exercises and gradually increasing the difficulty. It may be helpful to tape-record role-play sessions of meetings because in this way the main points contained in the notes can be checked with the original discussions. Students should be encouraged to omit inessential words as well as points which are peripheral to the main argument. As soon as possible the notes should be written up in order that the gist of what has been said is still fresh in the mind. Reporting back from notes gives an idea of whether they are full enough or not.

Maps and Plans. Rather than attempt to cover the whole topic in depth, it is best to work from the specific needs of the student (for example, "Where did the car crash?"). Sometimes a more general interest in maps may develop in which case other types of maps and their conventions can be introduced.

Work could be developed in the following areas:

□ Very basic language work, for example, 'up/down', 'left/right', 'North/South/East/West'.

□ The concept of scale needs to be understood. This may be introduced by the student drawing plans of the room he is in, or his house or flat, or his garden. These same spaces can be drawn to different scales to underline the point.

□ When introducing street maps, work from the known to the unknown, for example, trace routes from home to work, or home to the shopping centre. This will involve reading street names and possibly giving oral directions.

□ Practise recognising symbols and being able to find and read the key.

□ Practise using the index (alphabetical order) and being able to locate places by using grid references. A-Z street maps give useful practice in using grids.

□ With the help of maps (often available free from estate agents, motoring organisations, etc.), specific places can be marked and identified, for example:

— football teams in various cities

— particular shops or pubs in the locality

— known railway routes, where the names of the stations can be written on cards and put in the order of the journey. The London Underground system gives plenty of scope for this, as do suburban lines into main cities.

Part 3
Evaluation and Record Keeping

Who evaluates? - How and when do you evaluate? - What do you evaluate? - Record keeping.

It is sometimes easy to become so involved in day-to-day activities that evaluation either becomes forgotten altogether or is a rare, special event. In fact only by evaluating past work can future work be effectively planned. Looking critically at what you have done, noting the changes that have taken place and the things that have worked more or less well, can also point out new areas of work.

Who evaluates?

It is essential that both tutor and student are involved in evaluation. We have already stressed the importance of the partnership between students and tutors and it is vital that this partnership includes evaluation. If a student is actively involved in evaluating what he has learnt, what he is learning, and what he needs or wants to learn, this reinforces the belief that in the end the student is responsible for his own learning. Rather like learning to drive, the instructor sits in the passenger seat, the student *must* stay in the driving seat.

How and when do you evaluate?

Probably the easiest way to evaluate what has gone on is to talk about it, although before you can both expect to evaluate in an honest and constructive way, you need to have established a relaxed relationship. For instance, there's no point in asking a student in the second week to be openly critical of the teaching approaches! It is also important to be a good listener as this is the only real way to discover changes in the student's basic goal.

Evaluation needs to be a continuous process as aims and objectives are not fixed and may change over a period of time. Don't just leave it aside until you find the time, or it will get swallowed up in the end of session rush to get things finished off. Set aside a regular time for it — whether it is ten minutes of each lesson, or part of a lesson once a month.

What do you evaluate?

Put simply, you evaluate all the factors which influence learning. Tutor and student, by discussion, can decide on the main areas that are appropriate to the student's needs. You could jot down a list of the things you consider important for learning, like needs, interests, confidence, coping with mistakes, and ask yourselves questions such as:

- □ What does the student think he needs to do well?
- □ Is what we are doing relevant?
- □ Are the methods successful?
- □ Which methods are most/least successful?
- □ Who chooses the materials?
- □ Are we progressing at all?
- □ Are we progressing towards our goals?
- □ Are we gaining in confidence?
- □ What is my role as tutor?
- □ Who talks the most?
- □ Who chooses the subjects for discussion?
- □ Who decides what is to be learnt?
- □ Is there anything the student would like to go over again?

Record keeping

Keeping records of the work that has been covered and the planning of future sessions are inextricably linked. It obviously makes sense to record what you have done not just for it's own sake but to help any tutor who may take over from you. Often the records prompt the plan of work although any plans you make need to be as flexible as possible so that you can meet immediate needs like those of Ray quoted earlier. In fact it's best to make outlines rather than detailed plans bearing in mind the need to vary activities throughout a session. Although initially record keeping and lesson planning is often seen as a tutor's responsibility it is important to encourage students to take an equal part in both recording work and planning future topics. In our experience only if you are determined to involve students will these activities become shared allowing that few students will have the confidence to tackle everything immediately.

Some of us have found it useful to use record sheets — like the one below although you may find it just as useful to list a number of headings that suit both of you.

Weekly Recording and Planning Chart

Date	Work Done	How Did It Go?	Further Work
14th February 1980.	Checked letter to Jenny and copied it out to send.	Fine	Go on with looking things up. Practise spellings of 'right' words. Start new reading book.
	Practised alphabetical order— dictionary, Telephone directory etc.	Getting quicker at this. I feel I know my way round the dictionary better	
21st February 1980.			

Some Useful Books

For further ideas and suggestions you might like to look at some of the following:-

Adults in Education edited by Jennifer Rogers, published by BBC Publications.

Adults Learning by Jennifer Rogers, published by the Open University Press. Basic handbooks on teaching adults and adult learning.

BBC Adult Literacy Handbook, published by BBC Publications, 35 Marylebone High Street, London W1. A general background book.

Working with Words by Jane Mace, published by Writers and Readers Publishing Co-operative, 9-19 Rupert Street, London W1. Reviews and development of the literacy campaign, largely through the eyes of the students.

Reading, How to by Herbert Kohl, published by Penguin Books Ltd. A stimulating and provocative view of reading and writing.

Reading Development and Extension by Christopher Walker, published by Ward Lock Educational. Written for teachers in schools, it aims to put over the message that flexibility in reading techniques and critical reading should be encouraged.

Working Together – An Approach to Functional Literacy, published by ALBSU. Looks at how we read and gives useful ideas for using everyday reading material.

Helping Adults to Spell by Catherine Moorhouse, published by ALBSU. Gives a range of techniques for helping with spelling.

How's It Going? by Martin Good and John Holmes, published by ALBSU. Looks at different ways in which students make progress and suggests how tutors and students can together assess and record progress.

Directions by J Cooper, published by Oliver and Boyd. This publication offers useful ideas and activities for developing the skills of skimming and scanning.

Basic Skills You Need ⎱ by H Dobinson, published by Nelson & Sons. These books
English You Need ⎰ have ideas which you might like to adapt.

Some useful materials for use with students:-

Black's Writing Dictionary published by Black (A & C) Ltd. A very good introduction to using a dictionary. Layout is especially good, in terms of type face, spacing and grouping of words.

First Dictionary by Walter Wright published by James Nisbet & Co. Ltd. Closer to a normal dictionary, this gives a wider selection of words but without the distraction of Latin and Greek derivatives and abbreviations.

It is useful to have a selection of dictionaries to choose from and the following might add to your collection:-

The Progressive English Dictionary by Hornby and Pamwell, published by Oxford University Press.

The Oxford Paperback Dictionary published by Oxford University Press.

Penguin English Dictionary published by Penguin Books Ltd.

Chambers Twentieth Century Dictionary published by Chambers Press.

Your Move, published by BBC Publications. The tutor's handbook accompanying the BBC television series 'Your Move' contains a number of exercises for developing reading and particularly spelling skills.

Write Away, by R Lesirge and C Moorhouse, published by BBC Publications. A handbook for tutors, to accompany the BBC television series 'Write Away', it offers practical teaching suggestions for spelling and writing.

Pick and Choose, published by Broadcasting Support Services, 252 Western Avenue, London W3 6XJ. An envelope containing 22 separate sheets each concerned with a different area of need, for example, reading timetables, booking holidays, comparing prices, etc.

Social Sight Signs, published by Learning Development Aids, Park Works, Norwich Road, Wisbech, Cambs. LDA produce a range of materials for developing word recognition, including sets of social sight signs. Well produced and may be useful at the beginning stages of reading.

In the Picture, published by ILEA Learning Materials Service, Highbury Station Road, London N1. A pack of 20 large photographs each with an accompanying work card it aims to provide interesting material at a basic stage of reading and writing to help students develop comprehension skills.

In a Word, by Ivanic and Moss, published by MacMillan Educational. This is a spelling pack, intended for those who can read with confidence and who wish to work on writing and spelling. Work cards cover a range of topics and suggest how words can be used and memorised.

Keys to Form Filling, published by MacMillans. The layout of name and address is displayed in a variety of ways. The reader is introduced to each aspect of form-filling separately. The pages can be covered by libra-film and students can use washable OHP pens to practise the activity as often as required.

Handwriting, published by Nelson. A set of booklets giving handwriting patterns for copying practice.

Spirals, by Anita Jackson, published by Hutchinson Educational. A series of short stories written for adults and based on supernatural themes. Simply written but exciting and enjoyable for new readers.

Writing, published by the Federation of Worker Writers and Community Publishers. A good example of student writing.

The above three publications are examples of a wealth of student writing which has appeared in print over the past few years. These offer a valuable source of relevant reading material and can often spur others on to writing.

Everyday materials should also be kept in mind such as:-

Newspapers and magazines

Atlases
Road Maps of Great Britain
A-Z or Street Maps

Materials from various organisations, some of which will issue materials free of charge:-

Health Education Council

Office of Fair Trading

Travel Agencies

Post Offices

Banks

Index